I0624928

Live to Tell

Six Award-Winning Tales

Brandon Spars

Wayzgoose Press

Live to Tell: Six Award-Winning Tales
Copyright © 2017 by Brandon Spars

ISBN-10: 1-938757-33-5
ISBN-13: 978-1-938757-33-4

Edited by Maggie Sokolik
Book Design by DJ Rogers
Published in the United States by Wayzgoose Press

No part of this book may be reproduced in any form or by any electronic or mechanical means, including information storage and retrieval systems, without written permission from the author, except for the use of brief quotations in a book review.

Dedication

This collection is dedicated
to my grandfather,
Colonel Bernard A. Schmitz,
and all the other storytellers in my life.

Table of Contents

Preface

Brandon Spars unfurls himself when he steps onstage. In front of a microphone, his limbs energize and extend. His head reaches skyward. His eyes brighten behind his glasses. His entire body is involved with his live storytelling and it makes for a memorable kinetic experience. But to me, that is not what makes Brandon remarkable in the craft. For me, it's his voice.

I've had the pleasure of watching Brandon win a Moth GrandSLAM and a StorySLAM in San Francisco. Both times he exhibited great and seemingly effortless control of his voice—tone, tempo, and intensity. He loves reeling the audience in, fastening them tight to a story and leading them to a satisfactory conclusion. Since getting to know Brandon a bit, I have unscientifically determined that his skill in storytelling comes from time spent listening to his grandfather, who was apparently a master of tall tales, in Missouri. There's precisely the right amount of hyperbole and rhythm in Brandon's tellings, and I suspect it is something he absorbed or inherited. Live storytelling is not a precise art, to be sure. But it is one that demands sonic skill and a genuine love for an audience. Brandon has both and moreover, he is not afraid of being expansive in order to delight his listeners. I look forward to hearing more from him.

Megan Jones
Co-Producer of The Moth, Bay Area

Foreword

The following six tales were performed over the course of 2015 and 2016 as part of story slams held in the San Francisco Bay Area. Three of them were part of West Side Stories, produced by Dave Pokorny in Petaluma, and the other three were performed for The Moth, a non-profit organization devoted to the craft of storytelling. All of them received first place, except for the story "Once in a Blue Moon," which received third.

Each slam has a predetermined theme, and I used those themes as the titles for all six stories.

In each case, I had to boil a much longer story down to fit it into the five-minute time requirement for the slam. Certainly, many details were lost, and some of the characters are far less developed than they are in a twenty or even forty-minute version of the story. It might interest the reader to compare the version of "Pressure," included in this volume with a longer version of that story that was featured in the podcast B-Stories under the title "Dark Honeymoon over Missouri" (itunes.apple.com/us/podcast/b-stories/id984326292?mt=2). This gives the listener a sense of how a story will loop more than once through a pattern of action in the longer version of the story. In the longer version, one of the characters stabs a fish with his knife while seining on a creek for bait fish before he attacks the mysterious thing in the water trapped in my cabin. In the five-minute version, there was no time for the first adventure on the creek. The longer version also features the vacuum cleaner salesman, Corky, who made inflated claims about the power of his machines. I was hard-pressed to lose this, as I feel that the story "Pressure" really is about exaggeration. Both the vacuum salesman and the character Boobie exaggerate, which is then undercut by the fact that the true events of the story—the vacuum cleaner sucking itself in circles under the water—are harder to believe than their stretched claims.

In an even longer version of the story, I am able to tell the audience that my wife and I drove away with our first wedding present strapped to the roof of our car, a new vacuum from Corky. I tell the audience that if they are in the market for a machine, he will still tell you his vacuums are so powerful they will cause a drop in pressure so big it will make your ears pop, and that his vacuums can suck a gallon of molasses out of a carpet. "But now," I say, "he adds that his vacuums are so robust, he has heard from a reliable source that they even work underwater."

The five-minute versions, however, gain something that is not present in the longer tellings. These versions of the story are the most conscious of the audience and the requirements of the event in which they are told. Nothing is extraneous. The result is a pure and simple version of the story in which new complexities stand out. Rather than being about exaggeration, the story "Pressure," in its five minute version, is more about human folly—the folly of attacking a vacuum cleaner with a commando knife, and then the gullibility of those who look at a picture of it and believe it was a catfish. Of course, there is the even bigger folly of bringing a woman on a road trip to Missouri for her honeymoon!

These tales are fluid, constantly expanding and contracting, but there is a core to each one of them. In presenting the five-minute versions of the tales, I am presenting the bare core with the very deepest of the meanings brought right to the surface. One might ask the question if it would be better to write down the longer, possibly more literary version of these tales, but if you want this question answered, you will have to read the introduction that follows this foreword.

Introduction

Part I: Factual and True Storytelling

Storytelling forums such as The Moth require that the stories be true. My stories, admittedly, push this boundary. In fact, after a performance at West Side Stories in Petaluma, California, the host, Dave Pokorny, was approached by several members of the audience who complained to him that they didn't think that my story "It Takes Two to Tango" was "true." Dave phoned me personally to convey the concern, although he told me that he, himself, did not share the same skepticism. The result was that I spent many hours contemplating the story.

"It Takes Two to Tango" is set in Majuro in 2000, where I was living and working as an English teacher at the National College of the Marshall Islands. It was hands-down the strangest place I have ever lived, and Konsuma, the main character in the story is, again hands-down, the most outrageous person I have ever come across in my lifetime. When I tell stories about Konsuma, I say that he is the largest person I have ever met. When I have more time, I mention that it looks like he is built out of watermelons. His biceps are like round South American varietals; his thighs, county fair prize-winners. Is this where I lose the more skeptical members of the audience? Does he really look like he is built out of watermelons? Or, is it the events of the story in which he and the other outrageous character, a local witch named Isha, engage one another: he bellows and charges at her, and she rips her skirt over her head and drives him back with the ghastly sight of her hirsute mound of Venus.

The skeptics are not the first to protest at the outlandish claims I am making. At Berkeley cafés in the 1990s, my very best friends from graduate school would frequently try to stop me as I told them about Indonesia or Missouri, all places they had never been to and and people whose identities they couldn't possibly even begin with any sort of journalistic corroboration. They got tired of trying to stop me, and I would simply overpower them anyway with forceful insistence that everything was true... and I have always believed that everything is true. My friend Mark decided he would no longer try to stop me, but a part of him found it necessary to alert me as to exactly when he had a problem with the story. He settled for raising his boot at precisely those moments he found hard to accept. The result was that for about five years my informal storytelling became peppered with demands that he "lower the boot" because it was all true.

I suppose it was with the small amount of success in winning a few of the story slams I have attended that my stories fell under a bit more scrutiny. "True stories, told live, without notes" are the requirements, and if you are winning titles or prize money there is a more critical atmosphere. There is at least a shred of competitive spirit among the tellers and the audience. Some audience members are even formally cast in the roles of judges; they are not listening for the sheer pleasure of the story.

I think the biggest point of contention with storytellers is not so much the flowery language (did Konsuma's body look like it was built out of watermelons?) but with the basic plot line (did Konsuma get driven back by the horrific sight of Isha's loins?). There are some in the audience who equate truth with what a journalist would call "the facts" of the story. Nowhere was this more painfully clear than when Ira Glass of This American Life retracted a story told by Mike Daisey about the Apple assembly plants he visited in China. Mike Daisey had produced a powerful, compelling monologue that culminated in a man who was maimed at the plant holding Daisey's iPad, a machine he had spent his life assembling at the cost of his hand but had never actually seen turned on and operating. After the episode had already run, other NPR journalists looked further into the details, and many things about the story were called into question. Mike Daisey may have never visited the dormitories he described. The woman he spoke with may not have actually been fourteen and below the legal age to work in the plant. The translator was tracked down and asked about the man with the crippled hand. She didn't recall the encounter ever happening. And yet, in the conversation Ira Glass had with Mike Daisey, Daisey, even in the face of strong evidence otherwise, still insists that his story was true. He was, more or less, demanding that Ira Glass put the boot of skepticism back beneath the table.

Quite clearly, Ira Glass wanted an apology. It was obvious he expected Daisey to eventually break down and admit that he fabricated the plot... that he had misled the audience by stating that this was a "true story." This, however, was not to happen. Daisey insisted that this was the finest piece of work he had ever done, and that the piece as a whole was true. His only regret was airing the show on This American Life.

The interview was painful and tortuous. Ira Glass left long silences in the dialog to help create the effect that Daisey was struggling with himself. The discussion with the translator and with Mike Daisey was followed by an attempt to get at the real truth in a piece of journalism that employed reports from Apple and statistics from the factories.

So, did Ira Glass do a service to the world with his scrutiny of Daisey's monolog? Undoubtedly some would say that he did. The presence of toxic chemicals, the age of the women Daisey interviewed, the condition of the dormitories, and the numbers of members in the underground unions were questionable enough for Ira Glass to rebrand Daisey's work as "fiction" and not as a "true story." Ira was willing to concede the metaphorical, universal truths that Daisey's story revealed like a novel by Tolstoy, but not the status as factually verifiable.

I think the complaints that were lodged with Dave Pokorny about my story may stem from a similar conflict in expectations. Truth is multifaceted, and the journalistic truth that is required in a This American Life piece has as its first requirement that the facts be accurate. And there are many who attend The Moth and West Side Stories who may have, as their first requirement, that the facts be verifiable.

The Moth claims to be devoted to the craft of storytelling, and there is the assumption that this craft does not get in the way of these facts.

In crafting a story there can be the tendency to want to shift the order of things, to condense time— or expand it— to recreate dialog that may not even be close to what was actually said. In the case of "It Takes Two to Tango," the theme demanded that the conflict between Isha, the witch, and Konsuma, the maniacal giant, be central. I ended with the image of them in a sort of sustained dance with one another, which, for the first time let everyone else breathe a sigh of relief. We could move around the downtown area without wondering where Konsuma was. We could enter the supermarket without Isha assaulting us at the front. Or, we could just sit back and enjoy them as they danced a mighty tango with one another.

I don't recall ever sitting down in the 106 degree heat and watching them, and, in spite of the sense I give in my story, their outbursts of activity were followed by hours in which they were not preoccupied with one another. In that way, I did mislead the audience if I created the impression that they were going at it constantly for an entire week. However, I would never call what I put together "fiction," even though there are, admittedly, many things about the piece that could not be substantiated by an investigative journalist.

Something I would have liked to have added but did not have time for was the response by the community of Majuro. Isha was eventually taken back to her end of the island where she had family, and

Konsuma was put on a regimen of powerful tranquilizers. Thereafter, he was frequently found sleeping on the side of the road. Not fitting into the theme of "mighty tangos" was the response by the community, which finally took the action that they always wanted to take: they were able to approach him in his sedated state and provide him with food and clothing.

In the true spirit of telling stories, I want to share a story about "truth."

When I was growing up, every summer my family would go to Missouri where we kept a small cabin on the Gasconade River. My brother and I enjoyed taking the small boat up river, fishing, and exploring the warm green waters. There were snakes, gar, bass, goggle eyes, and catfish. Everything was green and brimming with life compared to the brown hills of California. The Ozarks remain, in my mind, the most beautiful place I have ever seen.

While my grandfather was alive, he was fine with us taking his boat up the river or down the river. We could go up Swan Creek or down to the Big Eddy. There was one rule, though: "Don't go up Brush Creek."

"Why?" my seven-year old brother and my ten-year-old self would ask. "Why can't we go up Brush Creek?"

That was when my grandfather would lean forward in his chair. Rather than explain the nuances of trespassing on private farmland, he told us, "Because there's Indians up there."

"Indians!" we shouted and looked at one another.

"Mean ones," he said.

I have to clarify that this was back in the seventies, and my grandfather was not a politically correct man. He meant that there were Native Americans up Brush Creek, and he told us they were mean to scare us so we wouldn't go up there. He would then launch into a story about how a road went through that area leading up to a spring, and not too long ago, a group of workers had been driving along that road at night and had fallen prey to those mean Indians.

"Did they kill the men?" my brother asked.

"Did they scalp 'em?" I asked.

My grandfather studied us, and we waited silently. "THEY SKINNED 'EM ALIVE," he bellowed. And, my grandmother would reprimand him, "Ben!"

There were so many things wrong with this story. First of all, there were no Native Americans living in Osage County anymore, but the real problem, of course, is my grandfather's racism. He had been born at the turn of the century, and had fought in two wars, and, I am not even sure he lived long enough to have read or heard more balanced views of history, which reveal that the Native Americans were not inherently violent and were the victims of Western expansion.

He went on to tell us how the car these men had been in was still there. It had been driven down the bank into the river, and the men's corpses were in the car. If you looked, you would see their expressions of horror and pain still etched into their skulls.

If the intent of the story was to keep us from going up Brush Creek, it worked for two more years. And then, on a hot summer day, my brother and I found ourselves working our way up the creek.

At every bend in that creek, we would expect to

see the old car. And, at every bend we would decide if it wasn't around the next turn, we would head back. "He's just making it up," I said to my brother. "There's no car... and... there's definitely no Indians."

We became a little less cautious. We stopped paddling and fired up the motor, but around the next bend, I cut it. We drifted speechlessly toward a pair of headlights, catching the sun as it filtered through the cottonwood trees. There was a car! It was black, and it was halfway in the creek. Brush had gathered around it from the higher water, but there it was. The car was incredibly wide... not like a Honda, or even a modern Chevrolet. It was some kind of Chrysler. The windows were smashed and the rear end of the car was actually buried in the bank, like it had been there a long, long time.

Our boat drifted toward the car. Two wide-eyed boys stared into the driver's seat.

We stopped doubting our grandfather for another two years, and his story held sway over us, forming boundary lines, demanding caution and respect for the river and its springs and tributaries. And then...

My grandfather died.

I don't have time to go into the details of his death and all of the sadness, but I will mention that with this sadness came illumination into some of his stories, like the one about Indians up Brush Creek. My grandmother had always let him go on and on to us with his tales and prohibitions, and we assumed from her general attitude of disapproval but her unwillingness to get involved that she just thought he was being his regular, old yarn-spinning self, but we were wrong about a couple things.

You might expect that she would tell us there were no such thing as “Indians up Brush Creek.” It turns out there is some truth in what he told us. That region was the site of one of the largest Osage settlements (Osage were members of the Sioux), and since that time, we have learned about archeological excavations that have placed Native Americans on those banks for thousands of years. They lived there all the way into the early 1900s, until they were moved to reservations. In fact, one of them was none other than my great-great-grandmother.

The car? The attack? Well, you’d be right about thinking that never happened, but there was more to that than just a big lie. That old car buried in the mud and the brush was actually my grandfather’s car. It never had run that well, my grandmother told us, and finally a mechanic told him to scrap it, but he wanted money even to do that. My grandfather was so ornery and cantankerous that he wouldn’t give the mechanic the money just so he could junk it. My grandfather figured he could do that himself, and so he pushed the car down that road along Brush Creek, and simply sent it down the bank.

“But we saw bones in there!” I nearly shouted.

“Skeletons!” my brother chimed in.

My grandmother said gruffly: “There’s nothing in there... go back and look.” Then softly: “You all were just under his spell... .” Her voice broke when she said this. She had been under his spell for sixty years.

That week we ventured up the creek and finally took a good look inside the car. There was nothing but a bunch of sticks and logs in there, and one turtle.

Life has its many ironies and, of course, my grandfather's outrageous sense of humor feeds into these ironies. About thirty-five years after the death of my grandfather, I took my children up Brush Creek, and I told them about their great grandfather and some of the things he would tell me. I told them about the "Indians up Brush Creek."

My six-year-old son, who was in the first grade, straightened up importantly in the canoe, and he delivered a lecture: Indians is not a proper way to refer to the indigenous people of North America. They are Native Americans. When Columbus called them Indians, it was a result of his ignorance of global geography. I thanked him for the history lesson.

Nonetheless, I could see both of their eyes widen as they studied the banks of this creek and imagined it as a bustling Native American settlement.

I told them about the car, and I told them how my brother and I had believed there were skeletons in the car. Our canoe glided up the still creek, turn after turn—it wasn't even as far as I remembered it. We almost passed it, it had become so buried by gravel and brush—but there it was—just a headlight and the front fender were visible. We got out to see if we could uncover it a little, but it was really buried. And here is one of life's ironies.

"Dad," Clara hissed. "There's someone here... ."

Byron and I wheeled around, and the three of us faced an old, dark-skinned man. He wore only a cloth around his waist. He held an exotic looking pitcher in his hand. Further up the creek, the long brown torsos of three other men were seen jutting out of the water.

We learned from this man, who was actually from the San Francisco Bay Area, that the farm that had bordered Brush Creek, and included the spring that is its source, had been purchased by a group of engineers from Silicon Valley and converted into an ashram, where more than thirty residents can come to stay on retreat. These men were gathering spring water from the pool just above the one with the car. A Hindu ashram in the middle of the Ozark Mountains! We chatted a bit about the Bay Area, the relative heat in Missouri, and the beauty of its waters. And then, the kids and I loaded up in the canoe and headed back downstream.

"Those were Indians," my son said knowingly.

Tales have a way of cycling back on themselves, revealing the ignorance of the times in which they are spun, while still preserving the seeds of the past, of illuminating the future. My grandfather had been factually inaccurate when he said there were Indians up Brush Creek. His story was fiction from 1976 until his death in 1979 and it would remain fiction until 2007, when it became verifiable fact.

However, I would argue, that the story was always true.

Part II: You should write that down!

I can't recall how many times I have been at a party or dinner when I finished a spontaneous rendition of a tale, and someone will ask me, "Why don't you write that down?"

I knew instinctively that the stories I was telling to groups of three or four people would not translate into the medium of a literary short story. That is probably because I think of my stories less as literary short stories than as tales.

The difference between these two genres can be subtle, and there are cases in which a work might fall into both. For me, however, there is one important difference, and that is the role of the audience. This difference for me does not exist in a live performance, but it does when a tale is written. Let me explain.

There is a difference between reading a piece of literature and having it read to you. When we read silently we are left to fill in so many details, such as the quality of a character's voice (resonant, nasal, gruff) or how the character is speaking (sarcastic, weary, wary). When someone reads to us, they do many of these things, adding volume, accent, tone—"color" essentially—to what is printed in black and white. When we read a work of literature, we "perform" the piece, whether out loud or in our heads, but, more often, a work of literature, unless we are on a car trip across the country, is read silently. And because of that, in literature, there are many cues given to readers as to how to "color" the scene. Discourse is qualified as weary or sarcastic or cold, and there is a distinct aim to paint a vivid picture so that two readers might have similar takes on how to visualize a scene. No matter how far "within or behind or beyond" their work the author withdraws, they are still present, and it is their work.

When I am performing my tales, I am hardly the indifferent author, paring my fingernails, as James Joyce once said of writers and their creations. My tales are in the first person, and during the performance I am, of course, insisting that the events actually happened to me. I lived in Indonesia; I lived in the Marshall Islands; my mother is from the state of Missouri. These biographic details make the tales mine and mine alone. But, if they are any good, they do something that a piece of literature does not do. They invite retelling, something that one could not possibly do with a work like Ulysses or even a short story. In the intermissions of the Moth StorySLAMs, audience members retell the stories that they enjoyed to one another, repeating things the storyteller did and said. Frequently, the hosts of the Moth Bay Area, Corey Rosen or Dhaya Laskminarayanan, will repeat a part of the story as they take the microphone and turn to the task of introducing the next storyteller. In this way, a tale becomes less the work of a single author and much more something like communal property.

This is especially true when the tales are written. The reader of a tale becomes much more akin to becoming its author than the reader of Joyce or James' prose. However lost in the prose a reader becomes, the work still belongs to Joyce or James and very seldom becomes something brought to life again by the one who has read it to one who has not. It can be spoken about, it can be discussed, it can be interpreted over a cup of coffee, but it is not retold the way a tale is.

And so, when a collection of tales is read, they should be read out loud, and, when they are unspeakably funny, or sad, or scary, that is when the magic happens—magic that I argue does not happen with literature—the reader of the tale and its author begin to merge. The reader becomes filled with the authority of the one who lived through it, which is why, instinctively, children know to ask their parents questions when their parents read tales to them at bedtime as if their parents were its creator, and, just as importantly, why parents know to answer the question as if they knew. And they do know.

The concept of high literature has marginalized the tale as less the product of an artist and more that of a craftsman. The Brothers Grimm were two of the earliest to commit tales to paper, creating the impression that tales came from all over the countryside and were the product of a German people, when in fact most of the fairytales belonged to several women as much as A Portrait of the Artist as a Young Man belongs to James Joyce.*

I am not saying that audience members of a story slam will return the following month to tell a story they heard and expect to win the slam. I am saying that a good story will stick with them, and they will tell it and retell it to their friends, the co-workers, to anyone that will listen, and then, something magic will happen. The story they heard will inspire another story.

While a junior in college, back when I didn't really know that storytelling existed, I took a semester off from my career as an organic chemistry major. I had been spending hours in a laboratory, and when I walked outside, I would see students beneath trees reading books and sitting with one another in cafés. I had a crisis, and went to the safest place I had ever known in my life, and that was the small cabin on the Gasconade River in Missouri. There, I lived with my eighty-year-old grandmother, who picked me up and drove me out of the city to the Ozark Mountains. As we crossed the 89 Bridge, there was the green lazy river, stretched out and waiting. Just like every year, my grandmother told me in her wavering voice, "Say hello to the river." I remembered all those years when I would arrive or leave, having said hello and goodbye to this big, sleepy green giant.

I had brought a box of books that my friends who were English majors had put together for me, and it wasn't long before I read Siddhartha, by Hermann Hesse, a book that I believe changed my life, or, at least helped me find my way. It wasn't the path of enlightenment or anything like that. The book simply dramatized something I had been doing all of my life, and something I needed to do more. When Hess' character Siddhartha settles on a river and becomes a ferry operator, giving passage to merchants, samanas, and brahmins alike, he becomes enlightened. However, a big part of his enlightenment involved his ability to speak to and listen to the river. I knew I had to do this. I had more to say to the Gasconade than hello and goodbye.

Sitting on the porch of our cabin was unsuccessful, and so I decided to really become close to the river, and that meant going to its source and canoeing all two hundred miles from the Arkansas border to this little house in the northern hills of the Ozarks. I will never forget watching the tail lights of our family friend's truck disappear down the gravel road. I turned and stared at the puddle I was about push the canoe through.

Most of the first three days consisted of my dragging the canoe through what was really just wet gravel. Listen to the river? Ha! I was swatting deer flies and cursing at it.

Here and there a creek joined it, and by the fourth day I was drifting and paddling... and listening. "What would it say?" I kept wondering. "What would I answer?"

A storm drove me off the water, and I took refuge under the canoe. When the storm passed I emerged from the boat like a turtle, and I laid my things on a well-trimmed lawn to dry. Even though I thought I was in Mark Twain National Forest, this had to be someone's property.

I sat in the sun, and let my charcoal, sleeping bag, and sack of potatoes dry out. I stared at the cold, clear water, and I imagined that this was connected somehow to the warm, wide green water that ran through Osage County and joined the Mighty Mo. "What would it say?"

That was when I heard a voice. Loud and clear. Right in my ear.

"She don't say much this time of year..."

I turned around and found myself face-to-face

with the property owner. He ran a canoe rental, and he invited me in for a cup of coffee. His name was—and still is—Rich Spahr.

That was the best cup of coffee I've ever had in my life. It warmed my bones, and it brought me out of my five days of silence enough so that my imagination could be fired by this man. He told stories, one after another. Most of them were about the river, though a bunch of them were about his one-eyed dog named Blue. He told me about how he had seen every inch of the Piney and the Gasconade, and how once he rounded a bend in his canoe and plowed right into a rose bush. "It was growing right out of the middle of the river, with big sloppy flowers hangin' on it like a bunch of wet laundry." He followed that up with another one about how he kept seeing these things moving on the bottom of the river. At first he thought they were turtles, "a whole herd of 'em marching down the bed of the river." But, when he pulled one up in his landing net, he discovered they were live grenades—a military exercise in Fort Leonard Wood gone awry, no doubt. And then, the happy bass. This bass kept swimming around his canoe, poking its head out of the water giving Rich a look. Every time Rich threw his fishing lure, the fish would go get it like a dog chasing a ball. Rich would take the hook out, and Rich swore it was giving him a big, broad smile.

Some of the stories had a point, and some didn't, or I just haven't realized what the point was. A lot of them had unanswered questions, like: Did he ever go back and see if the rose bush was still there? Did he keep the bass and fry it? Did the military come in and remove the grenades? I think I might have asked these questions, and he probably answered them, but I don't remember what the answers were.

But one thing every one of his tales had was an ending—and following that ending there was always a silence. Not a long one, but just enough of one. It is in that silence that there is an invitation, and finally I began to answer that invitation. I finally followed one of his stories with one of my own. That was the first time I repeated the story my grandfather had told me about "Indians" up Brush Creek. I told Rich about the car, and how my brother and I were sure we had seen bones in it, and then I told him how we had finally gotten a good, close look just after my grandfather had died. I ended with the words of my grandmother: "He just had you under his spell." Rich and I were both silent a minute. We both took the silence in, our heads tilted as if we were listening to it. The river wasn't more than a hundred feet in front of us, twinkling.

It might be stretching things a bit to say that in this way I heard the voice of the river. In one of those paradoxical twists that happen in both tales and literary stories, the voice of the river ended up being the silence that Rich and I would share when he had ended a story and just before I would begin one. It is a comfortable, inviting silence that assures you that you have stories worth sharing, and that when you tell a story you are sharing your very life with those who are listening.

After that, I began to visit Rich every year. I would reserve a canoe, arrive, and he would take me a few miles up just like I was a tourist from St. Louis. He never let me pay, though. And then I had a wife, and then children, but he and I would always find a way to sit on that porch and swap a few tales from our lives. Of course, I was able to add how the Indian ashram had been built up near the source of the creek, and how there now were actually Indians up there.

While you, the reader of this collection, and I are not seated on a porch overlooking a river, it is my desire that you see these tales as an invitation. I hope that when you close this collection, that when my voice ceases to speak and that silence falls over you, you are just arriving at the beginning. I think the greatest thing that could come of this would be if these six tales produced six more tales told by six different tellers. So, read them out loud as much as you can, and when you feel the need, change them. And, if something sparks in your head about something that happened to you, start telling that. Then the magic has begun.

* * *

**According to Valerie Paradiz in* Clever Maids: The Secret History of the Grimm Fairy Tales, *the lone sister, Lotte Grimm, her neighbor and friend Dortchen Wild, as well as the Hassenplug sisters, were the sources of the majority of their collection. The tales did not come, as they claimed they did, from a long, arduous scouring of the countryside and long hours with peasant families.*

1

The Fast Lane

It was July Fourth, and I was on a road trip with my daughter and son. And, my daughter kept reminding me how fast I was driving. We were in the central deserts of Nevada. I was in the fast lane; you go with the flow....

"Sounds like the lane of conformity to me," she had said.

We were on this road trip for her. She wanted to be on the speech team, and her speech coach said she could, if, over the summer, she wrote a speech about American car culture. I took her on this road trip to give her a more personal connection to the material.

We camped, and I wanted to surprise my still-sleeping kids with a good, outdoor breakfast. So I reached for the zipper of the tent, and I put my foot down out of my sleeping bag. And "Eeeeahhh!" A burning pain shot up my right leg. It went up and down my rib cage, and down my arm, and when I pulled the tent back, sure enough, lying in the sand, the size of a goddamn lobster, was a scorpion. It had bitten my foot through the tent!

My poor kids. My son was the self-proclaimed research assistant for his sister, and he was documenting everything. He held up his phone with a picture of the scorpion on it. "Dad," he asked, "is this going into Sissy's speech?"

I wanted to reassure him, but my leg was feeling pretty bad. I ruffled his hair, and I said, "You bet it is!"

But in the car, I wasn't so sure, and when I got reception, I kept Googling "scorpion bites." Most were harmless. One got my attention. The striped bark scorpion, found in Central Nevada, can kill a small dog....

"Dad!" It was my daughter again. "Are you okay?"

I was sweating. I couldn't feel anything in my right leg, and my lips were buzzing. "Yeah, I'm fine," I said.

"Then why are you driving so slowly?"

I looked at the speedometer, and I was going thirty-five miles an hour. Thirty-five miles an hour in the fast lane! I subsequently found I could drive thirty-five or one hundred and ten, but I couldn't cruise along at a steady seventy-five. I couldn't go with the flow. You cannot drive in the fast lane when you've been bitten by a scorpion. And maybe that's the takeaway message here.

Well, thank god for cruise control. In the next town, I navigated the streets with my thumbs. And, the only medical attention I could find was an ambulance, but because it was the Fourth of July, it was in the town parade. That didn't stop me from loping along, pounding on the glass, saying, "Yo! I have been bitten by a scorpion!"

The driver did take the time to roll the window down and tell me, "There's no treatment for scorpion bites. You just let the toxins work their way out."

Bam! Something hit my head!

When I went back to my children, it was under a shower of cups, cans, and garbage. Someone shouted, "Stay out of our parade, you moron!"

My poor kids.... My son held his phone at his side. He knew this wasn't going into his sister's speech. Or, was it?

There's actually a happy ending to this. My daughter changed her topic from an informative speech about American car culture to a humorous speech, which was actually a scathing review of all the dumb things I have done as a father—this being just one of them—and people seem to find that funny!

I don't mind. She's done really well. She's won awards, and prizes, and you just might say it is she who is now in the fast lane.

The Moth StorySLAM
The Freight & Salvage
Berkeley, California
August 3, 2015

2

Once in a Blue Moon

Some people think it is bad that the people of Bikini get pay-out money every year—not once in a blue moon but every year—for the nuclear testing that was done by the US on their island. Some think it has turned them into beggars—even murderers—for a couple thousand bucks.

Well, I lived in the Marshall Islands, and I always enjoyed the time when the Bikinians came from all over the Marshall Islands, filling the hotel for a week. I was always reassured that the money made a positive difference in their lives.

One year I began to see things differently.

It was the week the Bikinians had arrived at the hotel, and I took my wife and young daughter there for dinner. I went to the bathroom. I was at the hotel urinal when I heard strange sounds coming from the stall next to me. “Are you okay?” I asked. The strange thing was, I could see that the person was not sitting on the toilet. They were lying on the floor leaning against it like they had collapsed or were injured.

My heart began to pound. I began to imagine that I had stumbled on the scene of foul play—a murder perhaps....

As heroically as possible, I said, "I'm coming in!" and I kicked the bathroom door open. I surged into the stall but then I stopped because... whoa! What I was seeing was not fitting into any sort of schema for the human body... the head... the eye... the lips....

"I'm so sorry..." I backed out.

Just a few minutes later, we would have to leave. The man emerged from the bathroom and drifted across the floor like a float in a parade. He ended in the arms of a very old woman. She held him and rocked him back and forth joyfully. She must have been one of the original victims, and he was clearly someone who suffered from severe birth defects. My three-year-old daughter became so upset by his appearance that she ran crying to me and buried her face in my arm and would not stop sobbing for the rest of the night.

My colleague, a fellow American, wouldn't admit that he had been frightened, but he had been driving past the hotel when he caught a glimpse of the man, and he had been so gripped by his appearance that he had driven his car off the road and into the lagoon.

The paper reported the incident, and there was a picture of the man—the indirect cause of the accident. It was blurry, but you could still see the way his head sagged over his shoulder and completely covered the right side of his body. His eye was a pink stripe of flesh about a foot and a half long. It was his lips that really made a strong impression—they hung below the level of his waist like two, enormous black hoses.

For this man, the money was probably making very little difference.

The Bikinians left the island to go back to their homes—to Rongerik, to Enewetak, to Kwajalein—but not to Bikini Atoll, which, even after almost seventy years, still remains uninhabitable because of the radiation.

The hotel returned to the empty, sleepy place it was. Until the Bikinians can move back to their island, the only place they can gather as one people, to give each other the strength, the peace, and the comfort the old woman and the man were giving each other, is the hotel on Majuro. Once every year, at least for the Bikinians, must seem like once in a blue moon.

West Side Stories
Sonoma Portworks
Petaluma, California
January 6, 2016

3

It Takes Two to Tango

On the island of Majuro, lives a man who is so large it looks as though he is built out of watermelons. I lived on the island during a year when he kept the entire island off-balance and on their guard.

His name–Konsuma–is misleading because he does not go shopping—he goes chopping. This means he enters the only grocery store wielding his one possession, a machete, and he takes everything he wants.

Konsuma wasn't purely feared. People were actually fascinated by him. I once saw a group of children following him as he strode down the middle of the road. The boy came within inches before Konsuma wheeled around and bellowed, "Hooah!" The children screamed and ran, only to gather again and resume their game.

The only one who couldn't tolerate Konsuma was the store owner, who lost money on every one of his raids. Since there were no guns allowed in Majuro, not even for the police, the owner hired twelve men to drive Konsuma away with the use of baseball bats. Bruised and bleeding, Konsuma evacuated the downtown area and nursed himself in his growing heap of boxes and cans. Then, it was rumored that he had left the island completely.

It was only a month or so before someone new filled the empty space left by Konsuma. Isha was her name. Some said she was a witch; others, a crazy bitch. I tend to believe the former.

She took up residence center stage for Majuro: right in front of the supermarket. Once, I tried to do some shopping, and she stepped in my path, her hands poised at the hem of her muumuu. Her wild hair framed a single bulging eye, which looked just like someone had gently laid a boiled egg on her black face. I took a hesitant step forward, but that was a mistake.

She suddenly ripped her dress up over her head and charged. NO UNDERWEAR. The most upsetting thing was a hissing sound that issued from her. I did not stick around to find out what would have happened had I stood my ground. Nobody ever did. Some said the hissing was coming from her vagina.

Another showdown was inevitable. The store owner had assembled his troops. Everyone on the island gathered grimly as the men made their approach. She reached for the hem of her dress as they tightened their grips on their bats.

It came from behind us... "Hoooooaaaaaah!"

"It's Konsuma," someone shouted, and a cheer of distinct excitement arouse.

The men seemed to realize that Konsuma had relieved them of their task of a grisly beating, and they melted in with the spectators.

Konsuma and Isha seemed to immediately

recognize that their fates were entwined.

She fingered the hem of her dress like a pair of six shooters. He displayed and brandished his machete. The tension built.

All of us, except for Konsuma, knew what she was going to do, and yet it would still be a total shock and surprise to everyone. Just as he was about to descend upon her and presumably stomp her into the ground, she ripped her skirt up and came flying at him—and yes—I distinctly heard hissing coming from that woman's loins. It was like the hand of the Mother Goddess herself came forth and POP! Shot Konsuma rolling backward twenty-five feet through the white coral dust.

And so it began: to the cries of excitement from everyone, a game of chase, punctuated by bellows and hisses, but more than anything, intense concentration on each other.

It didn't last forever. No dance can.

But no one will ever forget the week or so in which we could move about the town freely. Hell, we could go shopping if we wanted to. Or, we could just sit back and enjoy it as Isha and Konsuma danced a mighty, mighty tango together.

West Side Stories
Sonoma Portworks
Petaluma, California
February 3, 2016

4

Leaps

Twenty-five years ago, I was a new volunteer English teacher in Indonesia. I was on a two-day bus trip from Jakarta to my post in Sumatra, and I was miserable. I was miserable because I was sitting next to an Indonesian woman my own age, and she had become immediately car sick and was throwing up all over us both.

Deep in the Jambi jungles of Sumatra, the bus stopped at an enormous outpost. I sat alone, cleaning my pants, intermittently shooting fierce looks, while the woman compulsively chewed on a squid the size of a plastic shopping bag.

Suddenly the whole place went crazy. "Ya!" the owner of the restaurant was holding a baseball bat. He seemed to be tracking something. A monkey was swinging from the supplies that were hanging from the ceiling, orbiting the restaurant like a small dark satellite.

Fate would have it that the monkey would drop right down onto the woman's table. The monkey reached for the squid, and I'll be danged if she didn't do the same thing that she did when I tried to take her food a few hours earlier. She pulled back. The monkey pulled harder; so did she. The other passengers gathered around her, shouting warnings and advice. She was confused. She kept pulling back.

The monkey simply let go of the squid, and flew into her face, gripping her head with all four of its paws. She staggered under its weight, then regained balance. Meanwhile, the owner was approaching with the baseball bat.

I was distinctly aware of taps and pushes from behind. A young man had a look of great desperation on his face. "Go to her," he said. "Help her."

"Why me?" I shouted.

Nearly in tears, a young man shouted, "Because she's your wife."

"Wife?" The very person I most despised in the world at that moment, and he thought she was my wife! Ahhh... it dawned on me. Back at the terminal her parents had been immediately anxious about her spending the next two days alone next to me, a tourist. They had even talked about switching her seat. If only I had let them. But I had grown indignant, and I told them I was no tourist. Even though I was just a volunteer, I told them I was a young professor headed to my new post at a prestigious university. The result was that I got such admiration and respect that a) she didn't move, and b) by the time the bus departed, from the perspective of the other passengers, we must have looked like one big happy family.

It was a combination of a hesitant step from me and a shove from the other passengers that sent me leaping into the path of the bat. I shielded not only the woman from the blow, but also the monkey, who took the opportunity to make a few quick pelvic thrusts, blasting hot urine mixed with greasy hormones into the woman's face, then launch itself into the canopy of merchandise, the giant squid trailing behind like a rag doll.

The poor woman. She lay at my feet coughing and sputtering. But my "springing to action" had transformed me. I was no longer the cranky, whiny newcomer I had been just a few moments earlier. I wasn't a college professor either. I was a volunteer. I would be this woman's volunteer husband.

In spite of my throbbing shoulder, I knelt down, scooped her up and, to cheers from the other passengers, I carried her to the bus, where I set her gently in her seat. As the other passengers nodded with approval, I wiped the monkey urine from her face. I picked squid tentacles from her veil that she had burped up over the two of us. I cared for her tenderly all the way to our destination, where, everyone's beaming smiles faded to looks of confusion and astonishment, as she bolted off the bus into the arms of her real husband.

The Moth GrandSLAM
Castro Theater
San Francisco, California
April 12, 2016

5

Pressure

I can't explain some of the things in this story, but it really happened.

My wife is from the islands of Indonesia, and for our honeymoon, rather than go to Hawaii, I thought it would be a good idea to take her on a road trip from California to the state of Missouri, where my family kept a cabin next to a river in rural Missouri.

Two things went wrong. One, my wife became quite sick, and by the time we rolled into the cabin on the river, she had a pretty bad fever. Two, when I opened my door, out poured water. Thousands of gallons of river water. Thousands of gallons more were trapped inside from a recent flood.

I rolled up my pants and waded in to see about draining the house. Then I stopped. From the back I heard a splash. Through the gloom, I caught the luminous glow of white foam on the crest of a wake caused by something swimming beneath the surface. Something big was swimming in slow circles. Instinctively, I backed out.

I did the only thing I could think of, and that was go and get a friend of our family. He was a former Marine who owned the local bar. His name was Boobie.

The next scene is like something out of a goddamn horror film. There we were in the water in the house with a net stretched between us, and that thing turned and started swimming right into the middle of the net.

That was when the third thing went wrong. I lost my footing and went down—down in the water—down in the water with the thing.

I rolled over onto my knees, raking the muddy water from my eyes so I could deal with whatever was going on, and three things happened.

The first was the thing. It began to rise up out of the water, a giant log of flesh, slick and striped like the body of a snake, but swollen and bloated as if from some mysterious expansion within. A howling noise filled the room.

The second thing was my new bride. She had wondered what was taking us so long, and came in, tottering down the stairs. But the magnitude of the situation must have been too overwhelming for her in her fevered state, and she crumpled and fell into the water. I surged over to assist her.

The third thing was Boobie. At first, I couldn't even find where he was, but then I caught him in the beam of my flashlight. He was up on my grandmother's pie safe in a crouched position that only a Marine can do. In his hand was his big, black commando knife. Then he was over it, then down on it. Then he pushed his knife into it and gave it a twist.

Bam. Explosion. And a gritty mist filled the room.

Now, there's a picture hanging in Boobie's bar. In it are me and Boobie, and propped between us is Irma. Draped from our arms is what he'll tell you is a giant catfish he caught in his hands and killed. But the beard on every farmer in that bar will begin to bounce up and down, because everyone in that bar knows that what is hanging from our arms is nothing more than a vacuum cleaner. It had been left plugged in and when the water came in something must have floated into it and bumped the power switch.

It had been going in circles sucking water in, building pressure for God knows how long until Boobie burst it with his commando knife.

Well, I still owe my wife a honeymoon. Every year, the pressure builds a little more to take her to where she has in fact always wanted to go—Hawaii.

The Moth StorySLAM
San Francisco Public Works
San Francisco, California
July 26, 2016

6

Memories

I lived and worked in Indonesia for six years. It was in Bali that I met a young girl and fell in love. She barely spoke any English, and I barely spoke any Indonesian, and so—naturally—we decided to get married.

On the day of the wedding, as we filed into her family's garden, where the ceremony was to take place, there was this awful, terrible screaming and yelling. That was because my future father-in-law had locked his own mother in one of the bedrooms. You see, years earlier, he had converted to Catholicism, whereas she, along with the rest of the extended family, like most Balinese, had remained Hindu. When she refused to stop preparing the offerings she considered necessary for any wedding, he banned her. He banned his own mother from her granddaughter's wedding.

My parents had made the trip out to Bali. My father, referring to the shouting, asked, "What on earth is that?" But my mother hissed, "Be quiet, Byron," Of course they didn't know the first thing about Indonesia, or Bali, or what was part of the exotic culture or what was, in fact, simply a dysfunctional family dynamic.

A Catholic priest had to be driven in from the city more than two hours away. He took his position in front of us all in the garden, and, with the grandmother still shouting from the bedroom, the ceremony began.

At a certain point, the shouting from the bedroom stopped, but that was when I began to hear a rustling sound coming from the bushes next to me. Through a gap in the foliage, I caught sight of an eye—it was the grandmother. She had escaped the bedroom and snuck in as close as she could so that she could make the most important offering for a Hindu wedding, which was the sacrifice of a live pig. Just as I was about to say my one line, "I do," a hosey squealing erupted from the bush.

Dug! Dug! My father-in-law was on his feet. He had not underestimated his mother. He gave a signal, and two men I had never seen before, and who had been at the ready, descended on the bush. But, all they succeeded in doing was let loose the hog, which rocketed out of the bush, right at the Catholic priest. He struck a dramatic pose of great terror as the animal shot past him looking for some portal of escape, but finding none, ran the perimeter of the garden, bleeding profusely from its throat.

"What the hell is going on?" my father demanded, but my mother was quick. "Be quiet,

Byron. You need to try to be more open-minded."

My father-in-law was black with rage. His whole body was trembling—and when that hog ran past him—Dug. Dug. The ground shook. His calf muscles pumped up and down his legs like dribbling basketballs as he sprang into action. And then whooooosh! We heard the swoop of his mighty leg. And pop! His foot connected with the hog just below the ribcage.

He tried to kick that thing out of the garden.

But, the hog didn't go anywhere. It flopped in the dirt, just in front of him, completely lifeless. All of the power of his kick had been transferred to the weakest spot, the throat from which it was bleeding, and a spray of blood shot out—all over the priest.

The priest looked at his hands, then his chest, then threw his arms open wide and began to wail. "Heeeaaaaah!" Everyone rushed to comfort him. I held my sobbing bride to comfort her.

My father-in-law locked himself in his bedroom, and didn't come out for three days. To this day, we cannot even speak to him about the wedding. It has become fixed in his memory as a total disaster.

My wife and I have learned to laugh about it more and more. Our bad wedding has resulted in many years of a good marriage, and we now have two beautiful children.

My mother, far from seeing it as a disaster, and, in spite of us telling her countless times to the contrary, has, over the years, managed to convince herself that the wedding had been fascinating and spectacularly choreographed. On our twentieth wedding anniversary, we had a party, and, to our horror, she stood up to give a toast in which she recalled what she thought was the climax of the wedding when everyone sprang to their feet and shouted with excitement as the grandmother made her grand entrance from behind the bush. Then, wiping a tear from her cheek, she added that she could only hope people will remember to include her in such a meaningful way at her grandchildren's wedding.

All we could do was assure her that we will try.

West Side Stories GrandSlam
The Mystic Theater
Petaluma, California
December 7, 2016

Links to Performances

The Fast Lane

youtu.be/kbz_qKMRq3c

Leaps

youtu.be/NfA4Hc8IQmk

Pressure

youtu.be/piaRLh_IblM

Pressure aka Dark Honeymoon over Missouri (extended audio version)

itunes.apple.com/us/podcast/b-stories/id984326292?mt=2

acast.com/bstories/minisode17-darkhoneymoonovermissouri

soundcloud.com/b-stories/minisode-17-dark-honeymoon-in-missouri

Memories

youtu.be/OxD7ZkpNe-w

Storytelling Exercises

1. Listen to the story "The Fast Lane." The theme for this evening was the same as the title of the story, "the fast lane." This story took a very literal interpretation of the theme, and it shared an anecdote about a road trip through Central Nevada.

- What are some other ways you could interpret the theme, "the fast lane?" What stories from your life come to mind?
- What other themes do you find in this story?

Try this activity with any of the other five stories.

2. Every story needs a beginning a middle and an end. Listen to the story, "Leaps." What parts of the story belong to the beginning? Make several bullet points. What parts of the story belong to the middle? The end? How do these three parts work together to form a satisfying story?

3. Read and listen to the story "Pressure." Where does the storyteller use gestures or postures to help illustrate his characters or their actions? Try telling an anecdote in which you strike a distinct posture to distinguish one of your characters from the narrator or the other characters.

4. Read the story "Memories." Find places in the text that require vocalization or sound effects from the teller. Before you listen to the story, try reading the story with sound effects. Then listen to the story itself. What did the storyteller do that was similar to how you imagined the sound effects? What was different?

5. Each of the stories uses figurative language to help the audience see or understand something strange or different. The scorpion in "Fast Lane" is compared to a lobster (assuming we are more familiar with lobsters than scorpions). In "Memories," the father-in-law's large calf muscles are compared to basketballs, which dribble when he walks. In "Once in a Blue Moon," the man's massive, swollen lips, something we may have trouble visualizing, are compared to a common household object—a hose.

Find other examples of figurative language used to describe the vacuum cleaner as it rises out of the water in "Pressure," or the way "the witch" grips the hem of her dress in "It Takes Two to Tango."

Finally, as you construct tales of your own, create a metaphor helping your audience to visualize the unfamiliar by comparing it to something everyone has seen.

6. A pause in a story is useful for allowing your listeners to reflect on something that you said, or to let the suspense build. In the live version of the story "Pressure," there is a long pause after the character Boobie plunges his commando knife into the mysterious "thing's" body. Then there is an outburst from the storyteller: "Bam! Explosion!" Much of the pleasure of a story comes from suspenseful moments such as this in which your audience does not know something and it waiting to find out what happens. Pausing makes the best of those moments.

Read other stories and look for moments in which the storyteller might pause to let the suspense build or allow something to soak in. Listen to the live versions of stories and note where the storyteller pauses. In a story that you are putting together, try finding a place where you might want to insert a pause for dramatic effect.

About the Author

Brandon Spars lived and traveled in Indonesia and the Pacific Islands for about six years before attending the University of California, Berkeley, to earn his Master of Arts in Southeast Asian Studies and his Ph.D. in Interdisciplinary Studies. Since then, Brandon has taught high school and college for more than twenty years.

The classroom has always been his storytelling laboratory where loud booms, bellows, whoops, and thumps are frequently heard. Two years ago, Brandon began taking his stories outside the classroom to compete in events such as the Moth StorySLAM. He won the Moth GrandSLAM held in San Francisco in April 2016 with his story "Leaps," included in this volume.

Brandon lives with his wife and two children in Santa Rosa, California.

www.ingramcontent.com/pod-product-compliance
Lightning Source LLC
Chambersburg PA
CBHW071223170626
46809CB00005BA/1908
* 9 7 8 1 9 3 8 7 5 7 3 3 4 *